Bare Naked

a n d

NOT ASHAMED

The Marriage Manual

Drs. Royal and Kimberly L. McClinton

ISBN 978-1-0980-2540-3 (paperback)
ISBN 978-1-0980-2541-0 (digital)

Christian Faith Publishing, Inc.
832 Park Avenue
Meadville, PA 16335
www.christianfaithpublishing.com

Printed in the United States of America

To every couple preparing or repairing
Marriage will work, if you work it...till death
Build strong with love

CONTENTS

FOREWORDS

I'm biased! There it is. I said it. As an intentional kingdom-of-God builder, a loving and devoted husband, a doting and investing father, and influential doctor of psychology, I recognize my own biases relative to how this book differentiates itself from others, the credibility of the authors, and the book's relative value to the reader. That being said, I believe it's important to preface this foreword by disclosing that the authors of this awesome read are my eldest sister and her husband, my brother-in-love.

It is also necessary to disclose that I, personally, sow into this very ministry. I sow into what I believe in. And I truly believe in the work that they have put in over the years to save marriages and nurture healthy marital relationships.

The unique experiences of the authors, who have informed their respective perspectives, are the reasons the reader should delve into this book. They married early, divorced, and remarried each other. They see themselves, each other, and other couples through different (and, perhaps, corrective) lenses. They understand order and hierarchy as specifically instructed in the Bible. They understand the importance of knowing, understanding, and loving God first. Then they understand the importance of knowing, understanding, and loving themselves. This includes healing old wounds so they can become "whole." This will, prayerfully, prevent them from unintentionally bleeding on their partner. Lastly, they understand the importance of knowing, understanding, and loving each other. This includes exploring "negotiables" and "nonnegotiables." It includes relating to extended family and friends. It includes reciprocity and the so-called platinum rule which essentially is defined as treating others in the precise way that they would prefer to be treated. This obvious divergence from the golden rule is key, as it places emphasis on having intimate knowledge of one's partner and their idiosyncratic wishes and preferences while prioritizing them.

The authors realize that being in relationship with another individual is difficult. Also, they realize and teach that successful marriages require more than just love. In fact, understanding that love is just one ingredient that is necessary for a successful marriage is critical messaging. Furthermore, they acknowledge that all of this is a process and it takes time.

It is these "gems" (and a litany of others) that the reader will learn, enjoy, and have an opportunity to implement into their marital relationship. If utilized properly, the lessons will be invaluable and help to sustain healthy relationships and well-satisfied marriages. Be well… Be blessed!

—Dr. J. L. Weems, 2019

*****

"To be or not to be?" is probably the only one question that seems to plague the minds of every individual no matter what road they are on. For those married or inspiring to be married, it happens to be the question that determines what steps we take for a lifetime covenant such as marriage. It is such a huge question to answer and one that is probably scary to say the least. This manual is one of the greatest and most timely tools I know to assist you in making the decision that could represent the greatest covenant relationship ever established on earth by our Father in heaven—*marriage*. Not only does this manual deal with the ins and outs of marriage from finances, struggles, vision, intimacy, and more; but it also deals with your personal life's history, your individual perspectives and truths, and those challenges that may come with your difference. This manual challenges you to be honest about where you really are in life and if you're ready and in a healthy state to embrace this God-designed covenant of love. Taking the time to go through this manual can save you a lot of heartache and time loss in your journey of life. It helps you plan for the future and prepare for your now. What a healthy way to receive great counsel and insight regarding a covenant that is highly valuable in the eyes of our Father and so important for the aspect of family on earth. My prayer is that you receive all that is packed in this manual! It'll help you make the decision "to be" a covenant keeper and to "not be" one who dishonors this God-designed specially tailor-made covenant partnership of love on earth between you and your love! Let's be a great representative of the covenant of God and love on earth!

—Psalmist Raine

*****

Being 'The Marriage Love Dr.' and 'Nurse Good Thing' we have traveled the world encouraging the truth of marriage, love and sex. We believe in being raw and real which causes people to be transformed by truth. The truth of marriage, the Spirit of marriage, character and charisma (Galatians 5:22-23); the Will of God for your marriage and the Fear of the Lord in your marriage are some of the key points that must be reviewed, rehearsed and reminded of to have success in marriage.

The wedding lasts from two–six hours; the marriage is a lifestyle. It is sad that we have put more planning and emphasis on those hours than the lifetime commitment. This manual will give you a framework in which to work for your new lifestyle. Our Spiritual son and daughter have continued with the baton of raw and real with added experience of divorce and the realities of avoiding this route. We remind you of some keys before you digest and engage this information… Be Joyful—Ecclesiastes 9:9—live joyful with the wife whom you love all the days of your life; Rejoice—Proverbs 5:18-19—fountain blessed rejoice with the wife, love every part of her; Be Friends—Proverbs 17:17 a friend loveth at all times; Enjoy the Sweet—Song of Solomon 5:16 Friend til the end. My spouse for life; my friend til the end.

We endorse this work and encourage you to embrace the learning of Bare (Butt) Naked & Not Ashamed and be transformed… ready for marriage.

—Apostle Louis S. Greenup and
Prophetess Karen Greenup

PREFACE

This manual is written to assist those embarking in the beautiful life of marriage. It is also for those who have been married and need a reminder of certain principles or any time a couple needs a fresh start. It is imperative that we really face the issues dealt with in this manual to have a somewhat clear view of things you will have to deal with or are currently dealing with in your marriage.

It's so interesting that we have requirements with many stipulations to get any other licenses, but to get a marriage license, there are no requirements for this lifetime commitment of operating. I emphasize the length of time of the license because of the vows included in the commitment. Yet there is no training, no simulations, no testing for your ability to handle the lifetime commitment of a marriage license. Neither are there mandatory continuing education nor testing required from the issuing agency. Yet we are constantly tested throughout the marriage.

We commend you for your decision to work through this book and pray that it equips you, prepares you, and opens your eyes to the reality of marriage, yet allows you to enjoy the whimsical parts of planning a wedding and/or living this married life. We would say to thine own self, thy mate, and God be true. If, while going through this manual, you realize you are not ready to be married, we encourage you to gain strength and do not go through with the wedding. We promise you it will save you heartache and many headaches. Please don't just punk out! Explain to your fiancée the "what" and the cause of "why" you are not ready or what you didn't realize about marriage. Be honest and prayerful.

If you are already married, we pray for your strength to endure and trust the process. Divorce is an unnecessary death. According to the Word of God, divorce is only permissible through certain circumstances. So gird up your loins and strengthen your core. We encourage counseling with accountability for both spouses. Get help and endure.

OUR STORY

We are writing to fulfill a mandate on our lives to build strong marriages. It is our belief that if you build strong marriages, you build strong children with ethics who are able to be children and grow up moderately and appropriately, well-balanced; and if they replicate the same, then our communities, cities, states, and nation will be a better place. We have lived this married life for over three decades. At year twenty, we divorced for four years. Whew! But God, how did we get there! *Well,* listen let us tell you about the story of two kids...

Normally ladies go first, but since I am the oldest I will tell my story first. I'm the youngest of five boys born in a two-parent household. My father was a pastor who studied all religions, following the principles of Baptist and nondenominational and was the breadwinner of our family. My father displayed his love for our family by moving us from the west side of Chicago to the south suburbs to give us a better life. My mother was a homemaker and Avon sales lady in the neighborhood. Life changed for our family when My father unexpectedly died from a brain aneurysm at the age of thirty-seven. I was at the tender age of seven. This change caused my mom to learn how to drive and go to work. I had to grow up and learn how to cook and clean, do homework, etc. most times without assistance. During that era, families did not take children to counseling—to deal with grief. As a result, I became very rowdy at school and a jokester; I was always jovial on the outside yet in degrees of turmoil on the inside, trying to comprehend the loss of my father. So much changed. Not only was I not able to see, talk to and learn from my dad; but our church closed, and my mom had to work various hours trying to keep food on the table. My older brothers were graduating from high school and moving on with their lives. My grandmother took all her grandchildren to church with her, first to her brother's church who was Baptist, and then she joined a COGIC Church where my family became very involved holding various positions for years. In high school, I played football and was very good at it. After six hard years, my mother got married, and another change took place in my life. My stepfather decided to move from the suburbs to the southeast side of Chicago. This transition was not too hard, but I had to prove myself to the gangs, so I did a lot of fighting and won great respect among the gangs, and I was able to get a position on the football team. I found ways of dealing with grief through football and the ladies, and still felt as if I was missing something in life. Then I met Kim when I was sixteen and she was fourteen years old.

My football team won the blue division championship in my sophomore year my skills and ability afforded me the opportunity to be scouted by different colleges, but because of my grades, I would have to go to a junior college first and then go to a university. I was offered the opportunity to go play at Triton and Eureka Colleges with the condition of completing one year locally and then transfer. Being a big football jock afforded me many opportunities with the girls—older and younger.

Well my story differs in that I am the eldest of five children born to a two-parent household. My father worked full-time, and my mother was a homemaker. My family was focused on education, always striving to achieve great honors in school to move to a better school. My father is a Catholic, and my mother a Pentecostal. This dynamic afforded me the opportunity to be very familiar with both denominations of religion and often caused tugs-of-war within the family structure. To be Catholic was high reverence to God, soft, solemn songs, repetitious, and quickly over. To be Pentecostal was charismatic, loud, different every week, and strict. As a child I was very talented musically and artistically, in business, and as a gymnast; and I was also smart in school but was more drawn to my artistic abilities than school. I did just enough to get by and not be on punishment. Life was challenging in that the family of seven lived on low income, and although we didn't have designer clothes, we were taught that we had enough with each other. Being the oldest felt hard; expectations and the demand to meet them were high. Homelife was strict as a protective measure to ensure a successful life, without the financial barriers of life—to be able to write our own tickets. I often felt like I disappointed the house objectives because my desire seemed to always oppose the desired road. In high school, I went to a public high school and took an international studies program… Great, that pleased the house, but I decided instead of physical education and home economics to take the Reserved Office Training Corp (ROTC) course… Hmmm, I don't think that was the house's favorite. I am a great swimmer and could've been on the school's swim team, But I didn't want to have to change for PE. I excelled in rank and in all the patterns taught for those on the way to the military. Exposure to drugs and alcohol was high as well as the boys. Special treatment was given to ROTC members because we served and represented the military force in the school. At least that's what we thought. I also joined the school's gospel choir and was one of the lead singers in the group.

The home rules were to come straight home after school, not look left nor right, be home on time, no diverting, no excuses, do homework, clean up, watch a little television, and go to bed. We were able to go to Bible class at a neighbor's home on Wednesday nights. This is when the struggle between Catholicism and Pentecostal became real. I was able to sing and express myself more and began to understand that I should live my life for Christ. The neighbor who became my godmother began a choir with the neighborhood kids and began taking us out to church engagements to sing. Man…this sparked passion in me. I learned to direct a choir, and I developed in these skills fast. I stopped going to mass and began going strictly to my godmother's church and then my grandmother joined a COGIC Church, and I began going there. At the age of fourteen I met Royal during Vacation Bible School, and it all took off from there.

Our passion grew, and we began to "go together." My parents opposed of dating until age sixteen as a rule but would allow Royal to come over and would allow me to hang out with a group of teens after church, especially when there was night service or a youth convention.

In June 1985, Royal graduated from high school, and in July, I turned sixteen. I was allowed to go on dates, and Royal would be allowed to pick me up for church and Tuesday night choir rehearsal.

Royal had a 1972 New Yorker. It was often called the Bat Mobile. Boy, oh, boy, if those wheels, front bucket seats, and backseat could talk, hmmm, yeah Kim, with and without you, we would be in so much trouble. Needless to say, nine months after my sixteenth birthday, I found out that I was pregnant. I called Royal immediately after getting my pregnancy results, and we developed a plan. Remember I was smart, and even though I failed my entire sophomore year due to nonattendance, I went to night school and attended school regularly in my junior year, made up all my required credits, and was scheduled to graduate from high school as a junior. So our plan was as I was planning to attend Northern Illinois University and Royal Triton, which were not far from each other, we would keep the pregnancy a secret staying at our schools and then Royal would transfer to Northern after the first semester and play football there and we would get family housing and live happily ever after.

Our plan worked for almost two months. No one knew in either family. I was preparing for prom and graduating in the summer because I had to complete English IV and one more elective, and Royal was completing his year at junior college and working at the school. He had the grades to transfer, and everything was working well… We were so happy making plans for our baby and life away at college until Memorial Day, Monday, May 26, 1986.

Royal and I had perfect plans for Memorial Day. We were going to a couple of family BBQs and were going to enjoy ourselves. It was the week of prom. My mom decided to cook breakfast for the family—pancakes and egg omelet… Oh, my Lord, the smell made me nauseous, and I didn't have any morning sickness previously, but I began to feel very sick. I didn't want to eat. I went to the kitchen and sat down to eat. I put one piece of pancake in my mouth and ran to the bathroom to vomit. My mom came into the bathroom and asked me if I was pregnant. Oh no! Our plans…what was about to happen? I couldn't hide it anymore. I was totally busted. I replied, "Yes, I'm pregnant." So two months later to the date on my seventeenth birthday and Royal at nineteen became husband and wife. One week later, I graduated from high school, and we began living this married life, expecting a baby, trying to figure out what to do, who we were, and what's up next.

Twenty years later, after three children, two houses, ten apartments, about ten cars, two abortions (one medically necessary, one selfishly), good times, bad times, bouts of cheating, in church, out of church, with money and bankrupt, family vacations, respect, disrespect, loving and fighting (fist fighting) one kid in college and two in high school, we divorced, split the family, and went our separate ways with our first grandchild on the way. Royal declared the divorce was an unnecessary death.

Although we did all we could to live different lives apart, we were always brought back together, so we decide to be friends. Our oldest got married, and we had to work together. There were some family deaths, and we had to work together. Our younger children graduated and went to college, and we had to work together. We really still loved each other as we would occasionally come together, but so much hurt resided between us that we couldn't work together.

After three and a half years of divorce, God began working. He caused us to work together again, and the lights came on. God began to audibly deal with Royal and heal my heart too. In February 2010, a board meeting was interrupted by a prophecy that told me that I could begin planning my wedding. In March 2010, Royal scheduled an appointment to have his taxes completed by me because he couldn't find the person that usually would complete it. It was that encounter that brought an awakening to God's plan and purpose by design. From that date on, Royal and I worked intentionally to find our rhythm. On September 18, 2010, we found our rhythm and remarried, declaring that with God we were all we needed to get by. Together, we have determined to work to build strong marriages, helping couples to work through issues to avoid the unnecessary death of their marriage.

Lastly, know this…marriage is not just a good idea; it's a God idea with purpose.

Let's pray...

Father, we bless You and honor You for the covenant relationship of marriage and for this present opportunity to start a new life together. We thank You for the opportunity to grow together and share in the many aspects of family and love. We pray for your grace to endure in honesty and truth, to commit all to You and that You will be with us now and forever. In Jesus's name, amen!

SELF-AGREEMENT

I, _____ (your name), am currently

☐ seriously dating   ☐ engaged   ☐ married

☐ separated   ☐ divorced   ☐ widowed

_____ I desire to embark upon this process to gain insight on going to the next level in covenant relationship, so help me, God.

_____ I agree to be true in my responses as it relates to my feelings and viewpoint alone unless asked about my desires for my spouse, so help me, God.

_____ I promise myself that this evaluation of relationships is worth exploring to better myself and my present situation, so help me, God.

_____ I agree to be open to the truth of God's word, so help me, God.

_____ I promise to forgive myself and ask for forgiveness when I recognize that I may have violated some covenant principles, so help me, God.

_____ I promise to forgive those that may have violated me in relationships, so help me, God.

_____ I promise to finish this process no matter how hard it may be, so help me, God.

_____ I recognize I'm worth it, and so is my relationship, so help me, God.

_____   _____

Signed   Date

CHAPTER 1

Married, Its Origin and Purpose

And God blessed them, and God said unto
them, Be fruitful, and multiply, and replenish
the earth, and subdue it: and have dominion.
—Genesis 1:28, KJV

Bare naked and not ashamed: *"And they were both naked, the man and his wife, and were not ashamed. Adam and Eve the first recorded couple is stated to have lived in a Garden of Eden in which they had been given dominion over all"* (Genesis 2:25).

We must understand that this relationship was established in a place which was to be eternal. It was literally the first human-to-human relationship created by God. During creation, God called all that he made good, inclusive of man. The first time he stated that something was not good was when he looked at the man and said it was not good for him to be alone.

God then created a woman out of the man. They stood before one another naked. In our opinion, nothing hidden, nothing broken, no lack, no offense, no defense... They were in their purest states. The word continues with the fact that they were not ashamed. In a pure state, there is no shame, no comparison, no deformation, no irregularity. There was nothing that caused any doubt nor disbelief, no shade...nothing.

Marriage is a relationship between two people, although imperfect, yet they see each other as perfect for each other without an out clause, deciding to do life together. This view or opinion should not change. Yet in our society, these principles are not taught, established, or known for that matter.

According to the *Merriam-Webster, marriage* is (1a) "the state of being united as spouses in a consensual and contractual relationship recognized by law"; (1b) "the mutual relation of married persons, *wedlock*"; (1c) "the institution whereby individuals are joined in a marriage."

Per God's design, it is a relationship between a man and a woman who together can produce attributes, cultures, inventions, and children. This relationship is the one that causes you to have fruit, and if blessed, your fruit will remain throughout generations.

This type of relationship is often referred to as *covenant*. Covenant says despite your actions, I will be here and our relationship will remain until death when we are separated. Covenant does not have an out clause, nor does it just break. This is one of the reasons this relationship represents the relationship between God and *his* people. No matter what man does, God has a covenant that if they accept *His* offer and come into relationship with *Him. He* will never leave nor forsake them. It is our belief that Father also made the relationship to resemble the Trinity—God the Father, God the Son, and God the Holy Spirit, who are One. When husband and wife come together, in HIS covenant, they become one according to the Word of God. To establish a covenant, there was consent, agreement, decrees, vows, promises, and the shedding of blood. Once established, the only way out was through death.

When considering marriage or in marriage, we must have a forward and transparent view. It is not enough to think how cute our babies will be if we don't create a life expectancy for them to inherit and live out. It is imperative to look at your mate for witty ideas, inventions, plans, goals, and then your children which will speak to your legacy. I find it amazing that the name alone for some families declare and demand certain respect. The Rothschilds, the Jacksons, the Bushes...there's an automatic expectancy that anyone birthed from this family line will be credible and will uphold the family name and its values.

For example, if we look at the Bible throughout the known world, the children of Israel were known for having the God of Abraham, Isaac, and Jacob on their side; and only when they could be defeated was it known that they were not in good graces with the Father. The world knew this and were terrorized because of it. They carried the name well and who they represented very well.

We emphasize the *naked* with bare because it is, in this day and age, very unusual for people to be completely transparent with one another. There's usually something from the past that has not been revealed. We believe this stems from the fear of being rejected. It is our belief that we should set a new precedence and love uncondi-tionally flaws and all. Truly, we must check our love meters. Do we love with conditions? If so, you may not be ready to be married. The vows you commit to cover every aspect of life…good and bad. If you promise to live in all scenarios, that means all scenarios—the good stuff and the bad stuff. We cannot pick and choose and decide to quit along the way.

Marriage is creating a family bond to have an impact in the earth. We were created to have impact, and together, you should be a force to be reckoned with. What we can tell you, if you aren't ready to commit your life, then don't. If you're not ready to sacrifice, then don't. If you're not ready to deal with challenges and differences of opinions, then don't. If you are not ready to go to different places and share with others, if your world only beats to your drum…save yourself the trouble—do not get married. However, if you are ready to serve and be served, if you are ready to think outside the box of your own self and accept someone else's ideas and evaluation, if you are ready to accept the differences of the other person without being swayed from loving them unconditionally, then we would say you're about ready.

Yes, we said "about ready." You can make your best plans, but until you are actually in the bonds of marriage and a mixed ball of life comes at you, then you will have to decide how you will deal with the situation. To help you get started, please answer the following questions. Please be true...there's more at stake than embarrassment.

Exercise

Please answer these questions individually from your truth (your own perspective, not your mates) and then come together to discuss your answers. Patiently and lovingly hear your partners response, especially differing points of view. Understand that our realities are different based upon our pasts. So...be open to hearing the answers of the other, and converse together to come to an understanding and resolution.

1. What is your interpretation of the meaning of love?

2. What does your picture of marriage look like? Be as detailed as possible.

3. What does your role of the husband/wife look like?

4. What does covenant mean?

5. Describe what your spouse's role looks like?

6. How many children would you like?

7. How often do you desire to have sex?

8. If you can be identified as a "blended family," please answer the questions below. Otherwise, go to question 11.

9. How do you view your new blended-family-to-be?
    ☐ His kid(s)   ☐ Her kid(s)   ☐ Our kid(s)   ☐ N/A

10. What type of relationship would you like to have with the child's(rens) other parent?

11. What is your idea of coparenting?

12. Do you have any obligations that could/do interfere with your marriage that you are not ready to deal with?

13. Are you an introvert or extrovert?

14. How do you best communicate?

15. How would you describe yourself?

16. How would you describe your fiancé/spouse?

17. Would you sacrifice your life for your fiancé/spouse?

18. Is your family supportive of your decision to marry your fiancé/spouse?

19. What are your thoughts regarding income?
    ☐ His   ☐ Hers   ☐ Ours

20. What are your thoughts of clean?

21. What are your thoughts on financial obligations?

22. What are your thoughts on individual worship and corporate worship for your family?

23. If there was anything you could change about your fiancé/spouse, what would it be?

24. Why are you choosing/have chosen to get/to be married?

Take-A-Ways... To Dos and Notes

CHAPTER 2

Project Togetherness

But if you refuse to serve the Lord, then choose
today whom you will serve. Would you prefer the gods your ancestors served beyond
the Euphrates? Or will it be the gods of the
Amorites in whose land you now live? But as
for me and my family, we will serve the Lord.
—Joshua24:15, NLT

Now we will do a project together, something like what you may have done in grammar school. We will create a vision board. Individually (separate from one another and without discussion) pick out pictures of your vision for your family within the next five years. Set a date to collaborate. Decide who will bring the poster board, tape/glue, scissors, and a picture of you all together.

Your vision should include things that you would ultimately like to see manifest within your life. The following categories should be represented as applicable, your family makeup, career, business(es), ministry, hobbies, home, credit, finances, physical aspects, health, travel, etc.

Before arranging your vision, set the picture of the couple in the middle of the poster, and then set the other pictures around it.

This project is to build your skills of working together. *Note, you may not use all of the pictures you bring to the table.* But if agree-able, you may. The objective is to be able to come to an agreement on things and then strive to reach them within a certain time frame.

Biblical References

This book is written for all people. However, we must have an understanding of how the relationship and bonds of marriage were established, its purposes, its rules, and its way. Created by love *Himself* (for God is *love*), the Father looked and decided it was not good for man to be alone (Genesis 2:18). So out of him, God formed woman… She had to be the reflection of him and the exact opposite of him all at the same time, so that from them they could be fitly joined together to produce the seed in him, incubated in her, and reproduced into another being.

God created man and gave him dominion, power, and authority in the earth to give identity and purpose. When God carved woman out of man to stand by his side, God allowed him to keep the giving portion, and she was to receive from him and produce and/or multiply what he gave. Our Father is beyond incredible in this created model of mankind.

He commanded them to be fruitful and multiply, creating children (like beings) as well as creating a replica of heaven on earth to expand *His* kingdom. So from *His* point of view, this relationship was established in an eternal place for purposes by *His* design and by *His Will*.

Because *He* is *love*, we need to know what *love* looks like. We can get a good glance of it by reading and digesting 1 Corinthians 13. I like to use translations of the word in the vernacular of today, that's raw and real. For this chapter, we will view it from 1 Corinthians 13:1–13, as stated in the *Message Bible* (MSG):

The Way of Love

If I speak with human eloquence and angelic ecstasy but don't love, I'm nothing but the creaking of a rusty gate.

If I speak God's Word with power, revealing all his mysteries and making everything plain as day, and if I have faith that says to a mountain, "Jump," and it jumps, but I don't love, I'm nothing.

If I give everything I own to the poor and even go to the stake to be burned as a martyr, but I don't love, I've gotten nowhere. So, no matter what I say, what I believe, and what I do, I'm bankrupt without love.

Love never gives up.
Love cares more for others than for self.
Love doesn't want what it doesn't have.
Love doesn't strut,
Doesn't have a swelled head,
Doesn't force itself on others,
Isn't always "me first,"
Doesn't fly off the handle,
Doesn't keep score of the sins of others,
Doesn't revel when others grovel,
Takes pleasure in the flowering of truth,
Puts up with anything,
Trusts God always,
Always looks for the best,
Never looks back,
But keeps going to the end.

Love never dies. Inspired speech will be over some day; praying in tongues will end; understanding will reach its limit. We know only a portion of the truth, and what we say about God is always incomplete. But when the Complete arrives, our incompletes will be canceled.

When I was an infant at my mother's breast, I gurgled and cooed like any infant. When I grew up, I left those infant ways for good.

We don't yet see things clearly. We're squinting in a fog, peering through a mist. But it won't be long before the weather clears and the sun shines bright! We'll see it all then, see it all as clearly as God sees us, knowing him directly just as he knows us!

But for right now, until that completeness, we have three things to do to lead us toward that consummation: Trust steadily in God, hope unswervingly, love extravagantly. And the best of the three is love.

Love Challenge

What are the places in love which you need help?

_____

_____

_____

_____

Do you understand love now? Let's see? Please answer these questions in your own language as it relates to the scripture.

1. If I flow eloquently in language but don't have love, what am I? _____
2. If I prophesy, have power, and reveal mysteries but don't have love, I am _____.
3. If I give all of me, am killed, but don't have love, I am _____.
4. My net worth is _____ without love.
5. Does love give up? ☐ Yes ☐ No
6. Does love just care for self? ☐ Yes ☐ No
7. Does love want what it doesn't have? ☐ Yes ☐ No
8. Love struts its stuff! ☐ Yes ☐ No
9. Love is swollen up and forceful? ☐ Yes ☐ No
10. Love always says, "Me first." ☐ Yes ☐ No
11. Love goes off, when necessary and when not? ☐ Yes ☐ No

12. Love keeps good records, dates, messages, etc. of wrongs? ☐ Yes ☐ No
13. Love puts up with anything? ☐ Yes ☐ No
14. Love, loves the truth, God, and never fails? ☐ Yes ☐ No

Our biblical reference is more than a moral compass; it is our guide through life with God as the Captain of our soul, navigating through the murky earth. So taking a closer look at the relationship of marriage, we find in a review of Ephesians 5:21–33 (TPT):

> And out of your reverence for Christ be supportive of each other in love. For wives, this means being devoted to your husbands like you are tenderly devoted to our Lord, for the husband provides leadership for the wife, just as Christ provides leadership for his church, as the Savior and Reviver of the body. In the same way the church is devoted to Christ, let the wives be devoted to their husbands in everything. And to the husbands, you are to demonstrate love for your wives with the same tender devotion that Christ demonstrated to us, his bride. For he died for us, sacrificing himself to make us holy and pure, cleansing us through the showering of the pure water of the Word of God. All that he does in us is designed to make us a mature church for his pleasure, until we become a source of praise to him—glorious and radiant, beautiful and holy, without fault or flaw. Husbands have the obligation of loving and caring for their wives the same way they love and care for their own bodies, for to love your wife is to love your own self. No one abuses his own body but pampers it—serving and satisfying its needs. That's exactly what Christ does for his church! He serves and satisfies us as members of his body. *For this reason, a man*

*is to leave his father and his mother and lovingly
hold to his wife, since the two have become joined as
one flesh.* Marriage is the beautiful design of the
Almighty, a great and sacred mystery—meant to
be a vivid example of Christ and his church. So
every married man should be gracious to his wife
just as he is gracious to himself. And every wife
should be tenderly devoted to her husband.

Read this passage carefully, God is so serious
about marriage and our vows. It is a precious covenant that, unfortunately, we have seen so many
mishandled it with total disregard since biblical days. *This is another thing you do: you cover
the altar of the Lord with tears, with [your own]
weeping and sighing, because the Lord no longer
regards your offering or accepts it with favor from
your hand. But you say, "Why [does He reject it]?"
Because the Lord has been a witness between you
and the wife of your youth, against whom you have
dealt treacherously. Yet she is your marriage com-
panion and the wife of your covenant [made by your
vows]. But no one has done so who has a remnant
of the Spirit. And what did that one do while seeking a godly offspring? Take heed then to your spirit,
and let no one deal treacherously against the wife
of your youth. "For I hate divorce," says the Lord,
the God of Israel, "and him who covers his garment
with wrong and violence," says the Lord of hosts.
"Therefore, keep watch on your spirit, so that you do
not deal treacherously [with your wife].* (Malachi
2:13–16, AMP)

So we see, God intended *His* covenant gifted relationship to be
purposeful, to stand out among other relationships, and for it to be a
source or a conduit of *His* acceptance of our offering.

Question: *To the man*, as God sacrificed *His* Son to die for us, what are you willing to sacrifice for your wife? *To the woman*, what are you willing to sacrifice for your husband?

TAKE-A-WAYS... TO DOS AND NOTES

CHAPTER 3

God in Your Marriage and Household

Can two walk together, except they be agreed?
—Amos 3:3, KJV

While in high school, I served in ROTC. I learned how to walk in rank, in tandem with my company and battalion. One of the most memorable occasions was our battalion being asked to march in a parade in downtown Chicago. Our team was so sharp and precise in our motions. We represented well and was handsomely acknowledged among our colleagues. It was then that I learned that in order for things to progress you need to work in tandem or collaboration with that which you are working.

After many years in marriage, I have learned that the same principles apply. As spouses, we have to be able to walk together without tripping each other up, thus defeating your progress towards your personal goals.

In chapter 2, we covered spiritual beliefs, which include allowing God to be in your marriage—involved in the decisions, starting your day, choosing to serve him, etc. It is my opinion that it is extremely important to worship together so that your home, family, and union will be on the same page. It also adds a hedge of protection for your marriage. What was your viewpoint when you answered the questions? Has your opinion changed?

I Luv God, you don't luv God, what's wrong with you? This is an incredible song by Erica Campbell of Mary Mary. You can groove to it and rock to it, but you never realize how real this question is as related to marriage. Each person's relationship with God is different... Some are more relaxed in their relationship others are more formal. It all depends on how you were raised and what equated your love for God.

We must remember that we cannot judge others relationship with the Father based upon our measuring stick. This statement in no wise gives the person the ability to live haphazardly and continuously in sin, but let the Father do the measuring based upon *His* written word.

Your spouse's desire to be in ministry or attend a ministry of your exact liking may be different. Let's not even begin to talk about if your spouse is not saved. This is certainly a discussion that must be engaged. It is crucial! You may not believe that it will affect your relationship, but I promise you it will. This subject is a magnet piece. It can draw you closer together or so far apart that you will literally fall apart.

Often, we are so blinded by the idea of love and marriage that we neither think about all the components of life within marriage nor what will keep it together. The prophet asked in Amos 3:3, "Can two walk together, except they be agreed?"

We will approach this from two aspects: as a couple who believes in God and one that does not. Let us address the later first. It is our belief that without God, you are without hope and life is filled with continuous mission impossible situations. Yes, there may be some victories that you may win, but there are some that will take your relationship clearly out. It's not to say that you wouldn't make it. There is a will in man to defy odds, but allow us to ask you a question: how much better would it be to have the definition of love on your side? The only true advocate that will see you through. How much better to have the creator on your side, not having to rely on your own wisdom to navigate this bonding of relationship.

For those in agreement and aligned with the Father, it does not mean that everything will be roses. However, you do have the greatest advocate, there is, on your side to help guide you through the road, mountains, wilderness, valleys, pits, and triumphs of life. It is definitely just a matter of submitting our will to *His* will. In our opinion, it is crucial to have the Lord on your side. *He* instituted the relationship of marriage with the design to engage with the couple to have the influences of heaven on earth. Truth is that *His* ways are not our ways; neither are *His* thoughts our thoughts.

With God on your side, you will be able to institute certain quality lifestyles that will help you in your marriage. As believers, it is our responsibility to love God and love *His* people. We should engage in lovingly seeing about our spouse, praying for them, interceding on their behalf, and seeking to hear God for their life.

For great success in our lives, we must spend time in prayer, corporately and individually. It is imperative that we seek the directives of the Lord on our behalf and that we submit to *His* instructions. The way we will know how to pray is checking in daily with our spouse. It makes no sense to pray amiss. We are wasting breathe doing that. It is important to know what their need and soul's cry is.

Our son-in-love shared a principle some years ago with our ministerial staff that we have adapted and encourage couples to use with one another. This exercise encourages daily communication or provides a way of checking in with each other. It is the PIES check-in. You ask your mate to check-in saying how they are doing physically, intellectually, emotionally, and spiritually. If they are honest with you, you will know where they are and how to pray for them. It is important to also recognize that one answer replies to your PIES check-in is a signal that something is wrong or there needs to be a follow-up question to get them to share their heart.

Worshipping the Father in heaven together eliminates conflicts that are otherwise sure to come. Being split in the intimacy of worship breeds division. There's nothing more beautiful than to see a couple praying for one another, seeking God for one another, and speaking into each other's lives concerning their destiny and success. There's nothing like seeing a couple serving together. It can create a stronger bond because they are spiritually connected and scripturally backed. In the book of Ephesians, it says, "Husbands, love your wives as Christ loves the church," there's a clear reference here that the spouses are engaging in worship together and understand the love Christ has for the church. The wife is safe obeying the husband as he submits himself to the Lord. So we encourage couples to worship together and grow spiritually healthy, prayerful daily, genuinely curious of their spouses' inner workings so that the home will be on the same page spiritually with God as the head directing the path.

Teamwork makes the dream work. We often hear this statement in organizations, sports arenas, and other efforts that rely on everyone's efforts to be successful as a team. A team is not just one person doing all. It takes a collaborative approach to be successful in marriage. Michael Jordan would have never won the first three championships if it was not for Scottie Pippen, Horace Grant, Bill Cartwright, and John Paxton, and never would have won the other three championships for Scottie Pippen, Dennis Rodman, Steve Kerr, and others.

The proportions of participation can vary based upon the situation. Most think it is ideal for there to be a fifty-fifty split; experience has taught me that this belief is a fallacy and is more so than naught an impossible feat. It generally is not based on laziness but on inability, being unfamiliar, or the situation is just not their strength. This is where, as a teammate, the other picks up the slack and vice versa when the shoe is on the other foot.

There's this old saying that confesses that "opposites attract" and "men are from Mars and women are from Venus"; just different. I believe this statement is true. As humans, we long to be complete in areas in which we are not. With a spouse, you should have someone who compliments your deficits—having each other's back and being the support system; supporting each other's purposes in life.

What's Your Truth?

Are there any deal breakers at this point for you? _____
_____
_____

Create a statement of faith for your household for each category.

- Marriage
- Family
- Church
- Children

Sample statement of faith: We believe there is one God, and we ascribe to *His* will for our lives. We will raise our family to serve *Him*. We will live balanced lives, supporting one another. We will only engage truths and not waste precious time on nonsense. We will give God, each other, and our family quality time to thrive in each relationship. We shall fulfill the vision of this house and trust God for it all. We will not endanger our marriage nor family through fruitless actions. We will remain until death do us part.

Take-A-Ways... To Dos and Notes

CHAPTER 4

Expectations: Your Thoughts of a Perfect Husband/Wife

> I opened to my beloved; but my beloved
> had withdrawn himself, and was gone:
> my soul failed when he spake: I sought
> him, but I could not find him; I called
> him, but he gave me no answer.
> —Song of Solomon 5:6

Who are you looking for?

If you never divulge your expectations, you may be sadly disappointed. Your spouse may be extremely loving and thoughtful, however, they will not know your full thoughts nor expectations without you sharing them. If you cannot articulate to them what you truly want, you will be perpetually disappointed and upset with your mate, and they will never understand why. For example, I thought my husband would get the hint—especially from all the TV commercials that one certain day of the year the husband buys the wife diamonds or from TV shows that the husband sends flowers to the wife at work and then they have a blissful night. Well, unbeknownst to me, my husband would check out mentally from focusing on all commercials unless they were sports related or comedy in nature. On those special days, I'm expecting and *nothing*! Like absolutely nothing! When I would get home in the evening…with a little attitude yet hoping… here again, expecting because of the fantasy in my head of how I equated he would display his love for me—*nothing!* Oooh, was I mad repeatedly, then disappointed, disgruntled and ultimately thinking he just didn't love me? I just couldn't understand why he refused to do things like this for me. Then one day, I was inspired and mustered up the courage to ask him why he never did things like that for me, and he said I didn't know you wanted anything like that. Hmmm, mind you this was years and years of this buildup of disappointment and resentment and he never knew, and I was the culprit.

You see, we can't have expectations of someone without letting them know that this shows me you love me. We have to say what floats our boat in order for them to have the opportunity to fulfill it.

So during our first discussion on this topic, I expressed my desire for diamonds. His response was, "I can't afford them." I was angry again because we got all the flyers with ninety-nine-dollar sales on them, and I know he can afford it. Again, I say it, but he never paid attention, even if I circled it. Then I said, "Well, I would love for you to send me flowers to my job." He said okay, and that was the end of that discussion. Well, a few months later, another one of those days rolled around, and he sent me flowers. First, to get the call from the receptionist saying there was a flower delivery was normal, but then she said, "They are for you," I was *so* excited. My God! I was on cloud ninety-nine thousand until the delivery person brought this little pot of tulips up. OMG! I was *so* angry. My husband called my job excited because he had fulfilled what I asked for, and I was angry, not impressed, like on total shutdown. To him, I didn't appreciate his efforts. To me, he just didn't love me… I was totally embarrassed. Mind you, my husband is one of those "it's the thought that counts" person…so not good. That day on my way home, I cried, didn't speak to him, and was just out of it. He was completely outdone because he thought he did what I asked. Literally, he did, but…tulips? After a few days of no communications, a heated discussion ensued, and he stated that I didn't appreciate anything he did, even though he did what I asked him to do. I began to reply, "You sent me a little pot of tulips, and am I supposed to be happy? I was expecting a big beautiful bouquet or a dozen roses, and I received a little pot of tulips." Light bulb! Oh, I was supposed to tell him what type of flowers I desired. Hmmm, I couldn't believe that he didn't know what I was expecting, but once again, I was not specific, and per him…he really didn't know, and he was getting what he could afford. Well, after that fiasco was over with years spent, I learned to be specific…down to color and height if I want something from him or to buy the flowers I want for myself. This special delivery of flowers was not evidence of his love for me. It was that I wanted the world to know that I had someone like everyone else who cared enough to show the world how much. This delivery was not the measure of his love, and I had to question myself if I was operating in the spirit of pride. Truth be told, I just wanted to feel special from my husband, and I wanted the world to see and know. So it was good but tainted. I thought receiving the flowers in a big display would say I was loved and appreciated and that I had this wonderful husband at home. I did not know how to express my love language, which is receiving gifts and acts of service. I also had to deal with the fact that I desired the public display for wrong motives. Lastly, where did this faulty thinking come from? I had to recognize that this issue that I was blaming my husband for was actually my fault.

Now I am of the opinion that if I have expectations of my husband, I have to clearly communicate them with specifications. After going through all that, gathering of information mentally, I have to question myself why I want this—if valid, ask him, if not, drop it or buy/do it myself. This relieves aggravation and takes the pressure off the husband without stretching the bounds of his responsibility as a husband to a wife.

From my point of view, a man does not have osmosis (the process of gradual or unconscious assimilation of ideas, knowledge, etc.). I am the type of man that desires specific information and I consider myself as being a realist. For example, when I was asked to get diamonds, I knew at the time that I could not afford to get the type of diamonds she desires; nor could I afford a monthly payment. I was not thinking of the $99 sale as real diamonds.

When she told me about the flowers, I felt that it is the thought that counts. I was not thinking roses. I was just thinking of having flowers that I could afford delivered to her office. In my eyes the tulips looked nice. Remember, it is the thought that counts.

No matter how you were raised, you were raised in different households, which means there are different realities from both parties. There are two different perspectives and two different worlds, attempting to merge what they thought worked, saw, or didn't see.

Reality check, every marriage must find its own rhythm. What worked or currently works in one household does not work in the next. Certain principles can be referenced, but how you use them will be up to the individual couple to figure out. You cannot be stuck in your fairytale, dreamland world of perfection, typically, that is only in one person's head. However, based on your collaboration of vision and goals you can work together to achieve something.

We recommend you read *The Five Love Languages* by Gary Chapman.

Something to think about: do you know...

What demonstrates love to your fiancé/spouse?

TAKE-A-WAYS... TO DOS AND NOTES

CHAPTER 5

Submitting to One Another

> To love at all is to be vulnerable.
> —C. S. Lewis

Let's read Ephesians 5:21–33 and 6:1–4 (ESV).

Submitting to one another out of reverence for Christ.

Wives and Husbands

Wives, submit to your own husbands, as to the Lord. For the husband is the head of the wife even as Christ is the head of the church, his body, and is himself its Savior. Now as the church submits to Christ, so also wives should submit in everything to their husbands.

Husbands, love your wives, as Christ loved the church and gave himself up for her, that he might sanctify her, having cleansed her by the washing of water with the word, so that he might present the church to himself in splendor, without spot or wrinkle or any such thing, that she might be holy and without blemish. [a]In the same way husbands should love their wives as their own bodies. He who loves his wife loves himself. For no one ever hated his own flesh, but nourishes and cherishes it, just as Christ does the church, because we are members of his body. "Therefore a man shall leave his father and mother and hold fast to his wife, and the two shall become one flesh." This mystery is profound, and I am saying that it refers to Christ and the church. However, let each one of you love his wife as himself, and let the wife see that she respects her husband. (Ephesians 5:21–33)

Children and Parents.

Children, obey your parents in the Lord, for this is right. "Honor your father and mother" (this is the first commandment with a promise), "that it may go well with you and that you may live long in the land." Fathers, do not provoke your children to anger, but bring them up in the discipline and instruction of the Lord. (Ephesians 6:1–4)

Now after reading this passage, you often find out that people have ignored the very first verse, and they go into a defense mode of specific positions in the marriage. Truth be told, this word of instruction from the Apostle Paul is really a beautiful act of surrender to each other, not a division of someone having dominance over the other and the other just being a walking mat.

Submit means "to yield, resign, or surrender to the power, will, or authority of another"; with the reciprocal pronoun; "to yield without murmuring" in the fear of God. We picture it as being gently kind to one another resigning to the will of the other—in other words, respecting one another. Paul specifies that we are to submit first to one another—that's mutual. He further expounds what the wives' submission should look like. It is a known fact that once a woman loves and commits to a cause or person, no matter what happens, she's the die-hard, knock-down drag-out committed. Her commitment should submit as unto the Lord because he (the husband) gets his directives from the Lord. He then explains to the husband what his love for his wife will look like. He tells the husband, "Here's your picture… As Christ loved the church and gave himself for it…you are to love your wives—Ephesians 5:25." If we were to parallel these two directives, submit and love parallel. Could it be that the wife's submission and the husband's love equate to one another as a work unto the Lord?

When we look at this scripture, we find that the husband's task is actually harder than the wife's. This scripture literally makes the husband accountable for demonstrating the Father's love for the world. This means *He* went through all extremes. This directive also causes the husband to seek the Father who is not seen. Finally, it causes the husband to know where he stands… He literally has direct access as it relates to the life of the marriage. If there are troubles, issues,misunderstandings the husband has a direct access, that is above, who can give the husband the strategy and plan to conquer the issue and comfort and love his wife. The strategy the Lord releases to the husband that he gives to the wife will answer her questions and will satisfy the needs she has, to be given to. The truth of reality is even in our body parts, she was made to receive from her husband. If she never submits access to receive, she will never birth anything, and her purpose will be unfulfilled.

This is not a humiliating position. It is an honor to receive the seed, incubate it, and multiply it; but it takes submission to complete this objective. It is an honor to receive a vision from the husband, incubate it, and multiply that vision…to make it good.

So we see here, submission is not a bad thing. It is a position of honor that requires the husband and wife to look to the right source. Husband to Savior, wife to husband, children to (mother) wife, it is our duty and honor to keep the order.

There is a pattern here: the Savior sanctifies her to set her apart as or declare holy, make legitimate, free from sin, purified. The husbands should love their wives as their own body… He is responsible for taking care of her as his own body—nurturing, clothing, feeding, grooming, etc. Because of his responsibility, he has to leave the comforts of home and make a new home with his wife with God as his head, and then they fulfill what God originally ordained them to be one flesh. All the while, the wife must remain as the receptor because she cannot provide her own seed. Because of the weight of his responsibility, she should always be willing to receive. Because of God's design, she should always be open and willing to receive from the husband that is always fulfilling his responsibilities unto the Lord. As the wife, our responsibility is to make sure he can keep his focus and his ear attentive to the Father.

The History of Family Is Important

Ask questions for information purposes; these will help uncover potential issues due to misconceptions.

Question	Me	Fiancé/Spouse
Household type growing up? Single parent, married parents, or blended family		
Family medical history		
Influences/aspirations		
Serious or playful household		
Number of siblings		
Peaceful and quiet/ tragic and dramatic		

Take-A-Ways... To Dos and Notes

CHAPTER 6

Love Is Commitment

For husbands, this means love your wives,
just as Christ loved the church.
He gave up his life for her.
—Ephesians 5:25

I choose to love whether I like you today or not!

We are living in a world that taints that which originally was pure and undefiled. We change meanings to manipulate our own will and way. We do that especially as it relates to love. Love truly has been distorted into an ooohwweee goooeeyyy feeling or a look; it can be fallen into or fallen out of but never really offered as a choice.

In the beginning of this book, we listed 1 Corinthians 13 as a key biblical reference for marriage. Within this chapter of love are sixteen aspects of what does and does not define love, and from all of the points, there's a choice to do them or not to do them. Therefore, love is a complete choice. We've got to face reality—you are not engaged because you fell in love. No, you made a choice to come into agreement with what was displayed to you. That's why you asked the question and awaited the answer. That's why you received a question and needed to provide an answer. When you fall, that's like not a good thing because you end up hurt. Falling normally entails being tripped or taking a misstep. So, no, I'm not falling in love. I choose to let you in my personal space and into my heart that will allow us to become one. Wake up, people. We have to make a conscious decision to love. The word says that we will fulfill all the law if we love God and love *His* people. That little two-letter word *if* says that we have a choice to make, we have to decide to love.

There are times when we have quickly given our choice to love based on someone meeting a criterion or out of desperation, not realizing that we can literally make lifelong decisions and commitments based upon these rash decisions and end up in a lifetime of struggle and trouble because our love was conditional. The will of man is certainly fickle. We can be madly in love one minute, and the next, we can be calling it a foolish decision and literally throw away what we committed too.

Yes, this is the chapter that calls you on the carpet to challenge your choice to love the other truly for better or worse, for richer or poorer, in sickness and health. We don't realize how worse it could be until we are in the thick of it and ready to quit. We must remember the sixteen points of 1 Corinthians when we choose to love. Oh, you didn't go through them yet? Okay, here they are...

Love is...

> Patient (*makrothymei*)—a remaining behind, a patient enduring
> Kind (*chrēsteuetai*)—full of service to others
> Not envious (*ou zēloi*)—is not jealous
> Not boastful (*ou perpereuetai*)—does not brag, is not arrogant
> Not puffed up (*ou physioutai*)—not inflated with pride
> Not acting unbecomingly (*ouk aschēmonei*)—does not act unbecomingly
> Not seeking the things of its own (*ou zētei ta heautēs*)—not self-serving
> Not easily provoked (*ou paroxynetai*)—not quickly stimulated or give rise emotionally
> Not keeping records (*ou logizatai kakon*)—no records of prior evils or offenses
> Not delighting at unrighteousness (*ou chairei epi tē adikia*)—not happy with sin, injustices, iniquities
> Rejoicing however in the truth (*synchairei de tē aletheia*)—celebrates the true reality

Bearing all things (*panta stegei*)—supports, take responsibility for, able to accept or stand up to

Believing all things (*panta pisteuei*)—accepts (something) as true, feel sure of the truth of

Hoping all things (*panta elpizei*)—a feeling of expectation and desire for certain things to happen for the good

Enduring all things (*panta hypomenei*)—suffer patiently, remain in existence, last

Never fails (*oudepote piptei*)—does not ever neglect to do something, is never unsuccessful in achieving its goals, or meet the standards set by; does not let down

Now take a deep breath! When you say you love anyone, not just your spouse, this is what you are signing up for, or it is what you are committing too. It is a heavy responsibility to love someone, yet it is a word that we so commonly throw around. I wonder if we truly knew the meaning of love and had to prove our love, would we give it so haphazardly and freely?

When we choose to commit to love on this level, there are rarely take backs, especially if both persons truly mean what they are saying. This little four-letter word is packed with power, expectation, as well as security and confidence for the person receiving the love. It should be truly cherished and fulfilled.

I would advise if you are not at this level of commitment to stop and put a hold on things until you can come to this place of *love* that you choose to offer someone. Be reminded that someone's life depends on you living out the definition of *love*, as provided by God himself.

Yes, this is beyond challenging, and it directly defeats the humanist approach to love and life overall. Yet we are more than able to fulfill and accomplish it because we choose to, we strive to make it happen.

Challenging Your Love Ideas

What do we believe love is? Answer the question for yourself, and then interview your mate for their answer. Write down *exactly* what they say. Evaluate your responses.

What is love to me?	What is love to you?

Take-A-Ways... To Dos and Notes

CHAPTER 7

Love Is Not

Husbands ought to love their wives as their own
bodies. He who loves his wife loves himself.
—Ephesians 5:28, NIV

Love is not the owweee goooey feeling that gives you the butterflies
in your stomach. It is not the definition found on your favorite TV
show nor in your favorite love song. Love is not abuse, misuse, aban-
donment, neglect, or manipulative. Love is not just physical; neither
is it just emotional, nor is it fantasy. *Love is real!*

I encourage all not to fall in love, for just as quickly as you fall,
you can get up and out of love. I understand the sentiment behind
the statement, but let's really look at what we are agreeing to. If we
fall, it is not typically looked at as a good thing. When falling, you
try to break or stop the fall to avoid hurting yourself. You immediately, or as soon as you possibly can, get up from the fallen state of
being. Oftentimes, I have seen this in relationships. We fall in love
and quickly stand up out of it and move around to someone else.
How can we commit to love and then jump out and freely give it to
someone else? This is why we have so many broken minds, hearts,
and homes. We need to be accountable to the love we shower all over.
Or better still, let's just understand what love means, and maybe we
will use a different term to identify the stage we may be willing to
commit to, if we are really not ready to commit to love.

We have to be willing to be true to the meaning of love and then
share it appropriately. It is too valuable to just be throwing around.

58

The Bible reminds us not to cast our pearls among the swine. This would be one of those times.

Love is not sex; neither does it equate sex. It is not able to be made by the physical aspect of coming together. Love is not things. It cannot be bought or measured by what is bought. Love is not uncontrollable. It is truly controlled by its holder and can be freely given by the person.

Love is not to be mishandled, for it is dangerous when played with or misunderstood. Our culture has tainted the pure meaning and essence of love. We have turned aside from looking at the truth of love and pursued the tainted passions of entertainment to measure love or even if we are being loved. Years ago, it was the soap operas that dictated love. Now it's actors and singers who are our image of love, and they are often totally confused on the issue themselves.

Activity: What's Your Truth?

How can you love better?_____
_____
_____

Describe how you want to be loved. Keep in mind if you don't know, neither will your spouse.

_____
_____
_____

TAKE-A-WAYS... TO DOS AND NOTES

CHAPTER 8

Thresholds, Pain, and Tolerances

*Put on therefore, as the elect of God, holy
and beloved, bowels of mercies, kindness,
humbleness of mind, meekness, longsuffering.*
—Colossians 3:12

What is your threshold of pain? How well do you tolerate pain? These are two questions that you must honestly answer for yourself and then be able to share this information with your spouse/fiancé so that they can understand what is going on and how to recognize when you need assistance.

The difference between *threshold* and *tolerance* is…a *threshold* measures the various levels of pain from nonexistent to excruciating, while *tolerance* is what you are able to handle before needing assistance. Within each, there is an aspect of pain physically and emotionally when it comes to marriage.

Have you ever wondered why there's a scale of pain from 0 to 10? I have, and what I have come to understand is that there are times when pain is expected because of a physical trauma or an emotional event, but how it is measured is based upon a person's ability to handle it. Tolerance for pain and endurance differ from one person to the next. Say, for instance, you get a paper cut; it may initially sting and bleed, you run it under water, get it bandaged, and keep moving, literally forgetting about it. Someone else gets a paper cut, and they are jumping and waving their hand and blowing the cut. We recognize the two huge extremes: the one who has little pain may feel like the other person is overreacting to the incident. However, that person could be feeling fire in their bottom. What if these two individuals are married, this could cause unnecessary problems or hair-raising, awkward silence if not properly aware of the thresholds of your partner. This can become a nuisance in the marriage.

Be aware that there are levels of pain physically and emotionally that have to be understood and explained. This will help those opposites to fulfill the need in each for compassion, sympathy, and the lack thereof.

Hear me, just because someone's tolerance for pain is low or not on your level does not mean that they are a punk; it is how they were created. We are different individuals with various levels of sensitivity and tolerance. I believe it may be fair to say, women are more sensitive emotionally, whereas men are more tolerant. On the other hand, men are physically more sensitive to pain, and women are more tolerant. Some may disagree, which is fine, however. From my experience, it is common for a woman to feel pained if talked about or if not spoken to, like ignored when men will not care one bit; and a woman can have a baby with no medicine while a man stubs his big toe or gets the flu will cry like a baby.

According to Jennifer Graham, professor of biobehavioral health at Penn State, College of Health and Human Development in an article states,

> A person's pain threshold is defined as the minimum amount of pain that evokes a report of pain. Pain tolerance means the time that a continuous pain stimulus is tolerated. "Some feel that men have higher pain thresholds and tolerance levels than women because they believe that men are tougher overall," she says. "Other people think that women have a higher threshold and tolerance, the reasoning being either that women have evolved to be able to cope with childbirth

pain, or that they have dealt with so much naturally occurring pain in their lives that they can handle anything a laboratory technician might dish out."

Despite these entrenched stereotypes, research into pain response has produced variable results, notes Graham. In animals, pain studies have had every possible outcome: males have higher tolerance, females do, and there is no gender difference at all.

"Human studies more reliably show that men have higher pain thresholds than women, and some show that men have a higher pain tolerance as well," Graham adds. Another way of thinking about these results, she points out, is that women show more sensitivity to pain.

There are several explanations for the variability. A woman's response to pain is affected by hormones, Graham explains, specifically where a woman is in her menstrual cycle when the painful stimulus is introduced. But there is no agreement about how, exactly, the menstrual cycle affects pain response. "Some studies report that women show more sensitivity during the premenstrual phase, while others report greater sensitivity at ovulation, and still others, following menses," notes Graham. "A few studies have shown no difference based on the menstrual cycle."

The socialization of gender further muddies the waters. How do society's expectations influence the way experimental subjects report pain?

"This question is really key," admits Graham. "Boys typically learn that they are expected to be tough and not complain about pain. One study, conducted by researchers at the State University of New York at Stony Brook, found that men reported less pain in the presence of a female experimenter than they did in the presence of a male."

But the most confounding problem may be the complex nature of pain itself.

"Pain is inherently subjective," says Graham. "We typically rely on self-report to know if someone is experiencing it." And it's tough to determine how much of pain is sensory and how much is influenced by psychological factors, she adds. "The limbic system of the brain, which is related to emotion, is typically active in response to physical pain for both men and women. In fact, looking at functional MRI, it can be difficult to distinguish psychological pain—such as that caused by social exclusion—from pain that is purely physical."

Sociocultural and psychological influences seem to have a greater impact than any inherent biological factor, believes Graham. Pain lights up our nerves and our brains in ways that are more alike than different. "Overall, I think it's important to know that men and women respond similarly to pain at a biological level."

"How much it hurts may depend upon who's asking" (Stevenson, 2008). As initially stated, in the interest of promoting healthy relationships, we would suggest having this discussion of how sensitive you may be emotionally and how you may react when pained physically. When these occurrences happen, every bit of sarcasm and pride needs to be put away and attention focused on your spouse's needs. Now, let's say your spouse could win an Emmy based upon their performance. Try not to be irritated by their disposition. Just crown them king/queen with your love and appreciation for the person they are.

It seems like mates are attracted to those whose households are totally different from theirs, and we notice that those who played the "dirty dozens" have tougher skin than those who come from households that did not. It seems that in most single-parent homes, children play the dozens without offense. Could this be that they are using this as a defense mechanism—laughing and making fun of rough situations instead of crying?

Be sensitive and aware of who your spouse is and where they have come from. Your play could spin off into a whirlwind of issues that may take years to recover. We are not saying don't be yourself, but We are saying investigate their tolerance. Quickly apologize if you offend, or try hard not to be offended, understanding that their play is just a language of love... Go figure!

Fighting Fair

Words are like balloons released outside. Once released, you cannot get them back. They continuously float farther and farther away from you. Now take a moment and imagine you have one hundred million dollars attached to the balloon string and it was released outside in the open air. How do you feel?

Arguments may happen although they don't have to. However, when in arguments, we must be mindful to not release the hundred million dollars that depreciates the value of our lifetime covenant partner. We can easily begin to tear down our spouse with our words. We encourage you to be fair when dealing with issues. Remember you are going to marry or are married to God's child. You will be held responsible by God for how you treat them.

Take-A-Ways… To Dos and Notes

CHAPTER 9

Dealing with Conflict

Be angry, and do not sin: do not let
the sun go down on your wrath,
nor give place to the devil.
—Ephesians 4:26–27

As mentioned before, you are two whole individuals with two different backgrounds and experience of dynamics. No matter how much you have in common, similar mind frame and thoughts, the reality of point of views may often differ.

Exercise: face each other, discuss what your view is on the wall you see, and let your mate do the same. Did your views match? If not, explain to each other your point of view. Note: in various situations you will face with one another, you will still see it from a different point of view. The real nugget here is to explain your point to the one you love (using the principal meaning of love), and they, in turn, should visualize what you are describing. If agreeable, acknowledge that "I can understand your point of view and accept it," or respectfully acknowledge that "I understand your point of view but disagree with it," and give your reason for disagreeing.

The truth of the matter is that we won't always agree; but using the principles of love, we will have to find an agreeable point, respecting each other, forgiving each other, and restoring each other.

It is ideal to deal with all conflict without heightened emotions. Emotions can cause little issues to implode into huge stressful and unnecessary lost moments of time that you can never get back.

How do you deal with conflict? This is a question that you must honestly answer and seek resolve or help based upon your answers. We must totally deal with our truths and our struggles. If willing to accept our position that because of past experience our tolerance levels may be more sensitive than others, we must become more aware and deal with issues carefully.

There are times that our views can be skewed. We must find a common moral basis of dealing with issues and then work around it with our experiences. Then we will be able to truly deal properly with issues. We can control our outcomes with handling situations properly.

"Be angry and do not sin; do not let the sun go down upon your wrath" (Ephesians 4:26). This statement is not a suggestion; it is a directive. The preceding verse tells us that we should put away lying and speak truth to our neighbors, for we are members of one another. The proceeding verse tells us to not give any place to the devil. When we do not properly handle situations, we give place to the enemy whose sole objective is to kill, steal from, and destroy us.

What better way to kill a relationship than to allow anger and lack of communication to rule. It must be our endeavor to avoid the pitfalls of the enemy. We together must strategically work together in our relationships to be at peace. When we disagree, we must come to the table of reasoning, forgive, let love prevail, and restore the broken connection before the sun goes down. I believe that it is important that we adhere to this statement. You never know when it will be that person's or your last moment on earth. Alicia Keys has a song that says, "Love me like you will never see me again." When we love each other, we live in peace with each other.

First Corinthians 15:33–34 also says, *"Be not deceived: evil communications corrupt good manners. Awake to righteousness, and sin not; for some have not the knowledge of God: I speak this to your shame."* Filthy communication corrupts, it is a form of destroying. One of the greatest lies ever told, that we learned as a child was …"stick and stones may break our bones, but words will never hurt us." It is ideal to not let the words of others to hurt us, but this is so not true. Many live their lives defined by people's thoughts, word, and acceptance of who they are. We will change who we are based upon the opinions of others. Many have been walked into the realms of mental illness and disease because of the effects of other's opinions on their lives. There is nothing more stripping or downgrading as the words of a spouse who you are the most vulnerable with that will hurt and kill the spirit of the person.

When conflict goes bad or goes wrong, it will tear at the fabric of a relationship. When husband and wife become one, you are knitted together, much like you will find in a unity sand ceremony. Once the grains of sand are blended together, it is more than challenging and nearly impossible to separate them. Conflict with your spouse rips you to pieces. Some of you are still with your spouse, but there's a snatching away that can cause all kinds of errors in your functioning properly. It behooves us to appreciate one another and work within the bonds of love to keep the love and relationship whole.

We do not in any way ascribe to not sharing how you feel or what you may be thinking or don't understand. We encourage you to do it without calling one another names, and attempt to appreciate the other person's opinion. The spirit of offense can easily creep into opposing views and cause the heart of emotions to rise quickly, unintentionally. Speaking from this realm of emotionalism can lead to name calling, slander, and blatant blow-ups.

Have you ever been in a discussion and it just goes to the left? Ever wondered why or how you got to that point when it was never intended. It happened because one of the two individuals is disagreeing, and one or maybe both allowed permission to be a gateway allowing the enemy to sow seeds or plant roots of bitterness to emerge; then all of a sudden, a blow-up. We must be more aware and more intentional of what we say, how we say it yet be open to our spouse's perceptions and truths of the situation. We must also be open to hearing true intents without suspicion or our own decision of their true feelings. God is faithful that *He* will reveal what is real and what is fake without us tainting it.

We would advise to put into practice, practical measures to handle challenging times. If the situation is beyond both of you and you cannot hear each other, we advise to get Godly counsel—specifically an outside third party to assist *both* of you in working through the issues. If just one person gets counseled and works toward improvement and the other does not, the efforts are fruitless, because there will not be the same understanding nor goals.

We all love our family, and they love us. Suggestion here: be careful on sharing your struggles with family unless they can handle it. Reality is in most cases that the couple will forgive each other and reunite, back in love, and the family will hold an ought against your spouse. This rips the family unity. Can you imagine during holidays and family functions, your spouse getting the side eye or nasty treatment? The family relationship and bond need to be protected. Get a mutually respected third party to help and save the family the drama.

Here are suggested steps to resolve conflict:

1. *Take a break*: develop a strategy to cool down from a heated discussion within fifteen minutes, and return with the intent to (1) understand what your spouse is saying, (2) to resolve the issue, and (3) mend brokenness.
2. *Be reminded:* this is the love of your life and not your enemy.
3. *No time stealing:* tackle the small issues as they arise. It is the small issues compounded that become huge storms that do damage on a relationship and literally steal time that you can never retrieve.
4. *Ask yourself:* is this issue worth it?
5. *Open your ears to hear:* listen to what your spouse is saying; acknowledge when you understand points and when you do not.
6. *Try to agree:* it is important to come to an agreement for issues prayerfully on the same side of the fence. Yet there are times when you will have to agree to disagree and move forward.
7. *Never let the sun go down on your anger:* this is an allegorical saying that doesn't mean the literal sun but when you close your eyes on the day. Before you go to sleep, make your resolve with your spouse. How will you feel if your

spouse does not wake from their sleep? Is the argument not talking, not loving, being mean and ornery worth it?

Most importantly, it is not important to get your point across. Take everything to God in prayer and watch the opportunity and realization of understanding come to pass immediately.

Take-A-Ways... To Dos and Notes

CHAPTER 10

Finances

For which of you, desiring to build a tower,
does not first sit down and count the cost,
whether he has enough to complete it?
—Luke 14:28

This is one area in which many marriages break up. There is not enough money; and it causes stress in the areas of always working for it or towards it, begging, borrowing, and sometimes stealing because it's just not enough. The flip side of that is there is too much of it; and it is mishandled or abused, may cause trust issues, and is used as a tactic of abuse to withhold from the other spouse.

When there is not enough money, there typically is one in the relationship that will become a workaholic to get out of the situation not realizing that they are tearing the relationship down. Yes, we agree, paying bills, school fees, food, bills, etc. is necessary. However, I encourage you to have balance, for there will come a time in which you will find yourself by yourself.

In situations where finances are plenty, you will often find a lack of trust. Hiding, especially when one is coming into money and for fear of lack, they hoard and become secretive…always stashing so that they are never without.

Can you withstand financial crisis? Of course, you can. However, it will require transparency and connectivity to work through it such as establishing a joint bank account and work out how your household will handle finances. We must advise that due to life, you must be willing to be flexible and adjust as life adjusts. Yes, we can plan well, but sometimes, life really happens and can cause major shifts that must be addressed. You must be willing to restructure accordingly.

Budgets are an exceptional help in this area because budgets can change based upon monthly expenses. This flexibility allows for adjustment to be made based upon what is due and when. Keep in mind, at times, this may be a major adjustment for your spouse. They may or may not have had to deal with the responsibility of paying bills and will, therefore, need some time to adjust or learn.

Some may be used to living on the edge by making late payments, having disconnection notices and paying a little here and a little there to skid by. If that is you, please know that not only is it for your betterment to pay on time, but it is more than okay to pay ahead of time. If you ever desire a house or to purchase a car from a firsthand dealer, then you will need to have credit that speaks of your worthiness.

Decide how you want to operate your household, but know the two are no longer twain but one. I hear arguments of some that feel that paying bills on time helps the company out. Technically, they are offering you services with the agreement that you will pay them for their services, be it, electricity, water, gas, security, Wi-Fi, cable, rent, mortgage, or vehicle. If they are upholding their end of the bargain, you should do the same. You cannot have and live for free.

Bank Accounts

It is our opinion that a household account should be established jointly to pay bills and take care of the household. Individual accounts are okay, but that should have stipulations. Your paycheck should go into the joint account, and then a specified amount that is agreed upon by both parties should be transferred to your respective individual account for personal items and/or plans. I would also suggest a savings account for the household to maintain goals with all parties contributing.

We recommend full transparency of all income, credit, and its sources. If this is a problem, there may be some other hidden issues or factors. If nothing is hidden, nothing will be broken (like trust).

Here is some advice:

- pay bills before time, and keep your names in good standing so you can accomplish some of the bigger goals in life because you have a proven track record (your credit report) that follows you wherever you go.
- Save some money so that there is a pot for a rainy day.
- Invest some money so your money can begin to work for you.
- Spend some money to satisfy a desire or want, reasonably and agreed.
- Ensure that you have life insurance, car insurance, health insurance, etc. A setback in any one of these areas could be detrimental.

Many feel they can go through life without insurance, and they take the risk. When issues happen, you are left to pay out of pocket or not have the repairs or replacement done which could be a catastrophe. If it involves others and you are responsible for it, you could be sued, and that which you have could be taken away from you to satisfy the person's claim. It's just better to be protected through insurance.

Investing

To invest is always a risk. However, those risks can payout greatly or hurt you tremendously. You must be willing and in agreement together to take a risk and direct funds accordingly. From property and land to stocks and bonds, all can be a great benefit to have and ultimately help you to be successful and retire well.

In some relationships, you may have one who is more willing to risk and the other who is conservative or doesn't want to risk anything.

We suggest you consult a financial consultant who can assist and who can thoroughly explain the pros/cons and weigh your options.

Investing is a biblical principle! You reap what you sow (Galatians 6:7–9). You give, and more will be given to you (Luke 6:38). He will give seed to the sower (2 Corinthians 9:10–12). He that giveth to the poor shall lack nothing (Proverbs 28:27). You can find parables in Matthew 25 regarding investing.

Bible patterns yield Bible results. We admonish you to not be afraid but allow strategy to be released in this area and as you are led by the Spirit of the Lord (righteously) invest. Remember you are blessed to be a blessing (2 Corinthians 8:9).

Should you need instruction to further develop your budget and finances, we recommend you use a credible source, such as Financial Peace University (Dave Ramsey https://www.daveramsey.com/fpu).

Take-A-Ways... To Dos and Notes

CHAPTER 11

Strengths/Challenges

There are three things that amaze me—no, four
things that I don't understand: how an eagle
glides through the sky, how a snake slithers
on a rock, how a ship navigates the ocean,
how a man loves a woman.
—Proverbs 30:18-19 NLT

When I am weak, thou art strong, oh Lord! Most believe that their spouse can not handle their challenging moments. Truth be told, we tend to hide those areas of challenge praying they don't come out to embarrass us. In the forefront or the back of our minds, we tend to think that we will be rejected by our spouse due to weakness. We need to be open and honest. If they love you, they will continue to love your flaws and all. This is the beauty of covenant relationships.

We are helpers of one another, and it is opportunities like these that help others grow. How beautiful it is to be a part of the growing process of our mate. We have to endure to keep their confidence and know how to keep their vulnerabilities safe, which means not exposing nor joking about those weak sensitive moments.

Can I be vulnerable with you?

Can I be strong and not puffed up?

Reflect on these questions and answer for your beloved. Please do not give one-word answers but fill the conversation with what if I/what if I cannot, etc.

Remember you *must* be true to God, yourself, and your spouse. If you are not willing to confess your weaknesses, you may not be ready for marriage, because it requires being naked in more than the physical aspect. If you are already married, you will need to ask for a restart in this area to share what you've been hiding without the threat of losing that person. This will require humility, sincerity, and prayer on your behalf and the offender's part. I must caution you the offendee, you must be careful not to take the side of having the upper hand as the other person is eating humble pie. You must prayerfully and quickly accept their apology. Remember with the same measure you give, the same measure you will be given (APK paraphrase of Matthew 7:2).

In an effort to banish the enemy of pride and embarrassment from your relationship, ask your mate to be vulnerable with you by completing the list below:

Strengths	Challenges

Take-A-Ways... To Dos and Notes

CHAPTER 12

Work

The LORD God took the man and put him in
the garden of Eden to work it and keep it.
—Genesis 2:15

Work is a subject whose acceptability of who works has been based upon cultural trends, as well as the economy. As the economy shifts, it seems to require more than one income unless one is a professional such as a surgeon or baseball player. This is a very different landscape from households just a few generations ago.

Questions to answer as you ponder:

How were you raised, in a ☐ traditional home or ☐ untraditional home?

Are gender roles important to you?   ☐ Yes ☐ No

It is important to understand the principle of working being necessary to live. The Bible proclaims if a man does not work, he does not eat (2 Thessalonians 3:10). How we work and when we work are contingent upon what we do with the gifts and talents we have been afforded. Yet, as stated previously, working is necessary; how you work is based upon your exploring and exploiting the gift or the measure of faith you were given.

You can work smart, or you can work hard. Your work can be laborious and bothersome, or it can be effortlessly joyful.

You see when you work your gift and it produces for you resources that help you take care of your family, you enjoy your work and endeavor to explore it more. However, if you never put your gifts to work and just take what is available for entry level, you will get stuck in a cycle of hating your job, yet because it gives you a paycheck at the end of two weeks, you become chained to it. You end up feeling like you are wasting your time. You mumble, groan, and complain. Your home and family begin to feel your bitterness and resentment. You feel unsuccessful. This is true because you obtained a job that was never intended to make you comfortable in life. It cannot be relied upon to set you up for your future, and it is never enough.

So we speak to you now prophetically to ensure that you are working your gifting, because that is truly where you will prosper. It is what you were birthed into the earth to fulfill, representing what the Father called you for in this space and time to represent heaven.

In today's world, it does not matter if you work from home, have a home-based business, or work outside the home. The way this world is set up now, you can make more money at home than if you are working outside with all its additional expenses of transportation.

This is a really good place to drop this sidenote. Some couples experience issues due to jealousy, self-esteem issues, and the like, due to their spouse's ability to provide and the others inability. It can become a place of pride as having the upper hand or being better than the other. This ought not to be so among a married couple. You must remember this is not a competition, your spouse is not your step stool, they are not your beating post, and they are not your rug. Never should they feel in competition with your job. Your work may provide the resources for the household to function, but coming together, you both agreed that you were working for the common good as a whole, not the upper hand.

Please also note, sir/ma'am, this is not your easy place to take advantage of and get fat off your spouse. Work effectively and together to create a well-balanced home.

Take-A-Ways... To Dos and Notes

Children

Children are God's love-gift; they are heav-
en's generous reward.4 Children born to a
young couple will one day rise to protect
and provide for their parents. Happy will
be the couple who has many of them!
A household full of children will not bring
shame on your name but victory when you
face your enemies, for your offspring will have
influence and honor to prevail on your behalf!
—Psalm 127:3–5, TPT

Reality check 1: Although they are precious and a mini-you, they
grow up and leave you for a life of their own. Remember when they
were ages three to six and they did not want you to do anything
for them anymore…we'll give you a moment… Hmmm, well, that
period comes again when they become grown, and this time, they
come back needing you for money, to watch their kids, to get their
car out the pound, and so on. Rarely do they come back just to be
your precious little baby.

Reality check 2: Your life cannot be centered around them!
We have seen parents fully commit to the dreams and goals of their
child(ren). Nothing is wrong with this, but at times, it goes to an
extreme. We mean their entire world is what the child wants to do,
what they like, and what they won't do. The child literally runs the
house. Oftentimes in this situation, the husband has either checked

out or is just as dedicated as the mom. Their schedules and their lives are totally built and surrounded according to their precious little one. This is a huge mistake; you must provide for a balanced life.

It is not good for your child to have everything they want. This will cause them to live with a false reality, because the world will not be that loving. Your child cannot just say anything they want to say; the world will not be that loving. A child cannot expect the world to treat them as you do; they just don't love them as you do. So we are obligated to teach them to love and respect themselves and others. Teach them to be well-rounded with family times, friend time, study time, alone time, bath time, praying time, TV time, playtime, dialogue time, etc. Teaching them that these traits will help them develop well-balanced. When you set boundaries for the child, they understand, and it helps you to be balanced as well because you get the opportunity to see your child in action in various settings. You may just see who they really are and may in fact need to correct some behaviors that you otherwise didn't know they had developed.

In blended families, the action of the child(ren) can really affect the marriage. Sometimes, it can put the spouses against each other. It can cause a literal divide in the house. When moms that were very involved in their child's life get married, she is now paying more attention to that mate instead of the child. The child can no longer crawl in the bed with the mom. This causes a resentment against the new husband, and competition brews to see who can win moms attention. This was not God's design, which is why we are to marry first and have children within that union. However, our world's culture and moral values have changed, and what was once not acceptable is very much acceptable, and the original morals are very strange and unusual although very right.

So since we are here...we need to ensure there is a clean transition in boundaries with your new marriage. First, you need to speak with your child(ren) about your decision to marry. The introduction of this event does not need to be a surprise to them nor just forced upon them. Sidenote: they don't have a decision in the matter; however, they should be included because their life/lives will be impacted by this decision because the household will change. The dynamics of the relationship and your availability may shift.

We encourage you both (you and your fiancé/spouse) to share plans, dreams, and desires for your new household inclusive of everyone. Share what the household will look like and their responsibility in making it flow properly. We would include to ask them what they would like to see and do and listen to how they feel about this new way of living.

Open communication within the family unit is absolutely necessary! Sometimes when the family dynamics change, the child could feel like they weren't good enough or that you're replacing them; so it will be crucial to debunk all those ideas beforehand.

Family! Blended and All

Dealing with the family structure outside your home can be a challenging piece. We've seen the differences in other areas of marriage, but family can be your biggest cheerleader or your worst enemy. Love them but, respect them but, visit them but, cherish them but… set boundaries that are clear and will not violate your immediate family. You see marriage changes the dynamics of all relationships. Your first responsibility is your immediate family (spouse and kids), your second are your parents and siblings, and everyone else comes afterward.

We have seen challenges with tight-knit families where there is a mother or sister who is used to directing and handling all your life issues, and now that you are married, they are out of a job. This needs to be discussed and not swept under the rug…before the wedding. As mentioned before, it is not in your best interest to tell your family everything. They may never see your spouse as you do. Protect all, and please do not put them against each other so that you can keep both sides.

Please review the following statements answering which scenario best suits you and your family's way of living in comparison to your fiancé's/husband's family. Side note, if you note any repeats, it's intentional: (1) to make sure you understand who you are with and (2) to make sure you don't switch up on who you are.

Description	You and Family	Mate and Family
Example: Eating Dinner at Kitchen Table or Anywhere Pets or No Pets	Kitchen Table Pets	Anywhere Pets
Eating dinner at kitchen table or anywhere		
Own bedroom or shared a room		
Politely excused self to pass gas or let 'er rip		
Played the dozens or high respect		
Fought often or quiet and peaceful		
Pets or no pets		
Laughter or peaceful		
Kool-Aid or juice		
Hot breakfast or cold breakfast		
Home cooking or fast food		
Hotel pools or backyard pools		
Ride to school or walked to school		
Humor in injury or great concern		
Homework or lifework		
Designer or Kmart specials		
Doctor or grandma's home remedy		
Apartment or House		
Open door policy or call before you come		

Don't limit just to these questions. Ask more as you think of it.

Take-A-Ways... To Dos and Notes

CHAPTER 14

Sex

Now, getting down to the questions you asked
in your letter to me. First, Is it a good thing
to have sexual relations? Certainly—but only
within a certain context. It's good for a man to
have a wife, and for a woman to have a husband. Sexual drives are strong, but marriage is
strong enough to contain them and provide for
a balanced and fulfilling sexual life in a world
of sexual disorder. The marriage bed must be
a place of mutuality—the husband seeking to
satisfy his wife, the wife seeking to satisfy her
husband. Marriage is not a place to "stand up
for your rights." Marriage is a decision to serve
the other, whether in bed or out. Abstaining
from sex is permissible for a period of time if
you both agree to it, and if it's for the purposes
of prayer and fasting—but only for such times.
Then come back together again. Satan has an
ingenious way of tempting us when we least
expect it. I'm not, understand, commanding
these periods of abstinence—only providing
my best counsel if you should choose them.
—1 Corinthians 7:1–6

Hebrews 13:4 says, "Marriage is honourable in all, and the bed undefiled: but whoremongers and adulterers God will judge."

Sex is the most controversial topic on earth, this act has so many meanings, good and bad. This act makes families, yet it can break a family. From God's perspective, it is in this act that a man and woman become one. There is definitely a binding together through this act more than physically. It involves the tying of the soul. It can be addictive, gratifying, and pleasurable. It is uniquely designed for the covenant of marriage. In the freedom of the covenant, it is so good. God made it so good!

Guilty free and undefiled, anyway we want it...just between me and my baby! Hmmm, excuse us for a few minutes.

Okay, we're back!

Now be honest, were you shocked that we went there? If so, why? We are ministers of the Gospel. We love the Lord, and *He* blessed us with an amazing ability to come together and satisfy each other and enjoy one another fully...without restrictions nor clothing...amen! There is no shame! Is there shame in using a can opener to open a can? When properly engaged, it fulfills a purpose. The marriage bed is to be kept undefiled. Sexual intimacy shared between husband and wife is reserved for that couple only.

So we encourage all the couples we counsel to explore every inch of your spouse's body. Take your time to make a mental note of every mark. Find their birthmarks. Find marks they didn't know they had. Lift their legs and flip them over. This is to *know*! You may ask what gives me this right, well, scripture says the husband's body belongs to the wife and vice versa. As the wife in our team, I have a closet with...let's say equipment...for teaching the ladies how to handle their special packages, well! We share that it is important for both husband and wife to enjoy each encounter with climax.

Sex was not only created for pleasure, but in Genesis 2:26, it says God *blessed it* and told them to be fruitful and multiply. Most people only look at that scripture and say, "Oh, we're supposed to have children." But God is multiplexed. When *He* makes a statement, it includes so much more than our feeble thought. During the time of release, ecstasy is high, but as you're coming down from your high, those are moments of creation. If you have the ability to stay and bask in the glory and create—create businesses, and answers to problems, which produces fruit birthed from your beings that will cause impact in your lives and in the lives of others. Stay awake! Naturally and mentally! IJS

We understand physically and hormonally that sex is a necessity for the body. It is a basic need. Yes, God designed it within the body to be active yet within the proper confines and proper handling. Sin has certainly perverted the beauty of God's creation. There are various drives. No one has the same. It is common for drives to increase and decrease with age at opposite timings. Just make up in your mind that no matter what I am going to satisfy my mate's need with cheerfulness.

Try new and exciting things to spark passion, fulfill fantasies from role-playing of Tarzan and Janes to *Dirty Dancing*, to flirting with one another, cook a meal together, and taste along the way (you may want to taste the food as well; it ensures it's not too spicy)!—as long as you do not violate the bonds of marriage in any way or invite others (people or animals or other stuff) things into the marriage bed. Let me take time to note here that sex should be explored in the couple's natural way. If you have prior experience, please remember you had to start somewhere, and your spouse should not ever be compared to another. The two of you should create your rhythm being open to learning what pleases the other. Have loving fun, yes, at times being clumsy and at other times being extremely passionate and intentional. Enjoy the intimacy, the height, and the sensitivity of the moment.

Understand the peaks and valleys. Age, hormones, disease, and the like can kill your drives. This being the case, we must be sympathetic to the one in distress. We must be supportive and sensitive to how they feel. On the other hand, the one in distress must be willing to get the help needed to heal. The couple together should be approaching this issue together, not hiding from the subject. What do I mean by hiding? You go to bed well after or early before your mate does to avoid contact or trying. Even through your exploring options to help, you still need to touch, hold, taste, and enjoy your mate.

That physical connection is extremely important. It can encourage healing knowing that you won't abandon them during this time.

Special note: please do not degrade or threaten your spouse for not being able to engage you. Love them through the challenge. It is a very sensitive area in life, and if not handled properly and supportively, it can cause emotional devoid.

TAKE-A-WAYS... TO DOS AND NOTES

CHAPTER 15

To Be or Not to Be?

When thou vowest a vow unto God, defer
not to pay it; for he hath no pleasure in
fools: pay that which thou hast vowed.
Better is it that thou shouldest not vow, than
that thou shouldest vow and not pay.
—Ecclesiastes 5:4–6

The Bible says it's better not to make a vow than to make it and break it. Here's a tough question that you must answer... Did you specifically pray for the person you are to marry, according to God's will? Psalm 37:4 says, "Delight thyself in the Lord and He will give you the desires of your heart."

In chapter 2, we asked what were your thoughts of an ideal perfect spouse for you; have you submitted those thoughts and ideals to the Lord? It is important that you know what you desire and that you request it from the Lord.

Desperation will cause a person to jump and run into a "settling for less" relationship just to fulfill an empty place just to go through the process of a wedding. We encourage you to bring to the Lord your specifics. Here are some areas to write your specifics and begin strategically praying regarding your desires:

What do I really desire in my spouse?
Father, I desire a spouse who
   Cleanliness in the Home_____

Cleanliness of the Body_____

Security_____

Cooking_____

Lovingly_____

Speaks_____

Loves my family_____

Drive_____

Credit_____

Ambition_____

Considerate_____

Prayerful_____

Sports Oriented_____

Jokes_____

Serious_____

Intelligence_____

Talkative_____

Silent_____

Biblically sound_____

Works_____

Educated_____

Same Likes_____

Travel_____

Feel free to add other items that are important to you.

Take-A-Ways... To Dos and Notes

CHAPTER 16

Living Beyond the Wedding

For the woman which hath an husband is
bound by the law to her husband so long as
he liveth; but if the husband be dead, she
is loosed from the law of her husband.

—Romans 7:2

We plan meticulously for our wedding day. The venue has to be just perfect—the food, cake, colors, seating assignments, flowers, and, oh yes, saying yes to the dress. That one day can be the dreamiest or the most detrimental if things don't fall into place. Yet beyond that, we oftentimes don't plan our lives. Without plans and goals, we have nothing to look forward to. An idle mind is a playground for the devil, so we want to encourage all to plan your life and submit your plans to the Lord.

Let us remind you of your vision board. Go back and fill in the blanks. Remember Proverbs 3:5–6, *"Trust in the Lord with all thine heart; and lean not unto thine own understanding. In all thy ways acknowledge him, and he shall direct thy paths."*

Proverbs 19:20–21 (KJV) says, *"Hear counsel, and receive instruction, that thou mayest be wise in thy latter end. There are many devices in a man's heart; nevertheless the counsel of the Lord, that shall stand."*

Now you do the work…

What would you like to accomplish, as goal markers?

Year 1:	Year 2:	Year 3:	Year 5:	Year 7:
Year 10:	Year 15:	Year 20:	Year 25:	Year 30:

Prayer

Father,

We have gone through this journey, to seek knowledge, understanding, and our truths. We submit our will and desire to your will because you know what's best for us. Father, you desire truth in the inward parts, and we have revealed them. Father, we now submit to fulfill your design for our lives. Father, let us know how to change what needs to be changed. Father, help us to embrace our partner and this new level of life in marriage. Help us to embrace your design and fulfill everything you designed for us together. Until death do us part. In Jesus's name. Amen!

Be reminded…what God has joined together let no man nor woman put asunder.

Take-A-Ways... To Dos and Notes

ABOUT THE AUTHORS

Royal and Kim married as teens in 1986. After many trials, tests, good times, and bad times, they now have the burning passion to help couples be successful in their relationship. Ultimately, they desire to reduce the number of divorces among couples who seek counsel prior to or during their marriage. Royal and Kim experienced divorce for four years and were divinely remarried to help others. The couple reside in Illinois. They are the parents of three adult children and one son-in-love, and they have twelve grandchildren. They both have a Doctorate of Philosophy in Theology and serve in ministry as the pastors of Life in Christ Family Worship Center International in the Chicagoland area, are the apostles/overseers of Pure Life Network, and are the creators and hosts of Bare Naked and Not Ashamed Marriage Retreats.

Printed in the USA
CPSIA information can be obtained
at www.ICGtesting.com
LVHW090925251023
761975LV00044B/892